Old Testament Disciples

A Bible Study Overview of the
Sixteen Major and Minor
Prophets of the Old Testament

by Robert L. Tasler

AUTHOR'S NOTE

The Bible references used in this work are from the English Standard Version, 2011 edition, an updating of the Revised Standard Version of 1971, published by Crossway Bibles. I thank my lovely wife for her proofing-reading.

ALSO BY THE AUTHOR

(Paperback and E-Book)

Daily Walk With Jesus
Daily Word From Jesus
Spreading The Word
Reflections
Murder At Palm Park
Matrimony At Palm Park
Miracle at Palm Park
Bobby Was A Farmer Boy

(E-Book only)

Country Preacher
Small Town Preacher
Immigrant Son

(Bible Study)

The Hopeful Disciple
The Called Disciple
The Practical Disciple
Old Testament Disciples

Table of Contents

Preface

When considering the topic of discipleship, one usually thinks only of Jesus' disciples or at least the meaning of "disciple" in the New Testament. A disciple is a student and follower of a teacher, someone more learned.

None of the sixteen Old Testament men in this study were prophets from their birth. They learned their role from God or from others God had instructed and brought into their lives. All God's prophets are, in this sense, first His disciples.

The first three books in this Bible Discipleship series dealt with New Testament writers. I decided to go back into the Old Testament and dig deeper for men who learned their tasks from God Himself and then delivered His Word to His people. The Prophets were a natural group to study.

Most prophets were called by God, but for a time in Israel there was a "School of the Prophets" at the time of Elijah and Elisha, perhaps the greatest of the Old Testament prophets. Those two unfortunately did not commit any of their thoughts to writing, but Elisha was a disciple of Elijah who was a disciple of God. These great men preceded the Major and Minor Prophets we shall encounter in this study.

One commentator states the prophets had three purposes: They were to be Preachers, Predictors and Watchmen. As Preachers they admonished and reproved the people, denounced sin, and called people to repentance, both Jew and Gentile. As Predictors they announced the coming judgment of God, His deliverance, and events relating to the coming Messiah and His kingdom. As Watchmen, the prophets warned the Jewish people against apostasy, that is, falling away from their covenant relationship with God. This seemed to happen constantly.

I would suggest a fourth purpose, one more fundamental. The prophets needed to believe in the one true God of Israel, trust Him to do what He told them to do, and then go do it. That's what a disciple does. He believes and trusts God and then attempts to live what God says. Following those principles, the Old Testament prophets were true disciples of the Most High God.

This Bible Study is written to give the modern-day disciple an overview of sixteen prophetic giants of the Old Testament. All the prophets encountered in this study had their books included in the Jewish Bible. While the Major Prophets wrote lengthy works, most of the Minor Prophets are short, eight of the twelve containing four chapters or less.

While I encourage the use of several Bible versions, in personal study I have only used the English Standard Version in these sessions which can be used for either group or individual Bible study. May God bless all who read Old Testament Disciples.

+ *Rev. Robert L. Tasler, 2014* +

TIMELINE OF THE PROPHETS

There are sixteen prophetic books but seventeen books listed below, as Jeremiah also recorded his Lamentations. This elementary timeline gives a general idea of when the prophets lived and links them to the Gentile nations influencing Israel and Judah.

Shortly after Solomon's reign, the nation was divided and ruled by separate kings. "Israel" is the northern half of the nation and "Judah" the southern half. They were also conquered at separate times.

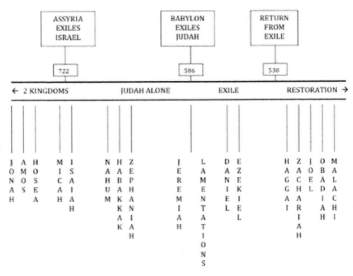

	TO ISRAEL	TO JUDAH	TO FOREIGN NATION
ASSYRIAN AGE	Amos (760) Hosea (760-730)	Isaiah (740-700) Micah (737-690)	Jonah (770)
BABYLONIAN AGE		Habakkuk (630) Zephaniah (627) Jeremiah (627-580) Lamentations (585) Daniel (605-530) Ezekiel (593-570)	Nahum (650)
PERSIAN AGE		Haggai (520) Zachariah (520-518) Joel (500) Malachi (433)	Obadiah (500)

Dedication

To my friends and former members at Epiphany Lutheran Church, Castle Rock, Colorado, especially Garry Fuller and the faithful servants of the Orphan Grain Train for their tireless work in helping clothe the needy.

"Old Testament Disciples"
An Overview of the Major and Minor Prophets

Session 1: Isaiah, Old Testament Evangelist
+ + +
THE PROPHET

Isaiah was born in Jerusalem 700 years before Christ, and had a 60 year ministry to Judah, from 740 to 680 BC. His name means *"God is salvation."* He and his wife, the "prophetess," had two sons, Shear-Jashub, (*"A remnant shall return"*) and Maher-Shalal-Hash-Baz (*"Spoil quickly, plunder speedily"*). He was one of several prophets who named his children for God's coming judgment or mercy. Isaiah prophesied mainly during the reign of King Uzziah.

The book of Isaiah is divided into three sections, chapters 1-39, 40-55 and 56-66. The first part is primarily a book of judgment, not only upon Judah (southern kingdom) but also on the foreign nations of Babylonia and Egypt. The second part speaks of the coming consolation and God's offering of forgiveness. The third part is about the divine nature of God Himself.

Isaiah's account of how God called him to serve comes in chapter 6 as he paints an eloquent word picture. *"I saw the Lord seated on a throne, high and lifted up,"* amid the praise of angels saying, *"Holy, holy, holy is the Lord of hosts."* The prophet eagerly responds to God's question, *"Whom shall I send?"* with words that sound like a true disciple, *"Here am I. Send me!"* Chapter 6:1-8 is the record of Isaiah's call to be a prophet.

THE ISAIAH SCROLL

In the late 1940s, Arab Bedouins discovered the Dead Sea Scrolls. Among the first items found was a leather scroll nearly 25 feet long made from 17 sheepskins sewn together. They sold the ancient scroll, not realizing it was a nearly complete book of Isaiah dating from 200 BC, 1,200 years before the oldest known Hebrew Masoretic text. That copy was located in Russia and known to have been copied around 1,000 AD.

Scholars compared the Isaiah scroll of 200 BC with the 1,000 AD text, assuming there would be significant differences due to copying. Instead, they found the two texts nearly identical except for some slight variations in spelling. The accuracy of the two copied Isaiah books attests to the care of the scribes in not altering a single word.

THE BOOK

Isaiah has three sections, and despite some modern scholarship to the contrary, all of them point to the same author, Isaiah. Here again is the basic three-part outline of Isaiah:

Part I – Ch. 1-39 – Judgment on Judah
Part II - Ch. 40-55 – Comfort for God's People
Part III – Ch. 56-66 – God's Divine Nature

In writing his many words to the people of Israel, Isaiah foretold the virgin birth of Jesus, whom he refers to as *"Immanuel,"* that is, *"God with us"* (7:14). Commentator August Pieper calls Isaiah 53 the greatest of all chapters of Isaiah and perhaps the entire Old Testament. In it the prophet depicts the Messiah as the suffering

Servant: *"But he was pierced for our transgressions; He was crushed for our iniquities; upon him was the chastisement that brought us peace, and with his wounds we are healed."* (Isaiah 53:5)

Passages from the book of Isaiah are quoted about 120 times in the New Testament. As the Gospel writer John noted, *"Isaiah said these things because he saw his glory and spoke of him."* (John 12:41) Isaiah is undoubtedly the most prominent of the prophetic books. His general purpose was to comfort God's people with the Good News of their redemption through His mercy and grace.

Martin Luther urged his people not only to read Isaiah, but to follow its advice and instruction. Though he didn't expect the people to understand its contents well, he wanted them to read the prophesies and admonitions that pertain to the coming kingdom of the Messiah, Jesus Christ, *"the savior of those who have gone before and those who are yet to come."* (Lectures on Isaiah)

Part I - Chapters 1-39: Judgment on Judah

1. Look up these passages. Where have you heard them before?

a. Is. 1:18 _____

b. Is. 2:4 _____

c. Is. 9:6 _____

d. Is. 11:1-2 _____

e. Is. 17:10-11 _____

f. Is. 30:18 _____

g. Is. 37:32 _____

Part II - Chapters 40-55: Comfort for God's People

2. What do these passages tell us?

a. Is. 40:1-2 _____

b. Is. 40:3-5 _____

c. Is. 42:1-3 _____

d. Is. 52:7 _____

e. Is. 53:5-6 _____

f. Is. 55:6-9 _____

Part III – Chapters 56-66: God's Divine Nature

3. What do these passages tell us? Have you heard them before? How might we apply them to our lives today?

a. Is. 56:1 _____

b. Is. 57:14-15 _____

c. Is. 59:14-15 _____

d. Is. 60:1-3 _____

e. Is. 61:1-3 _____

f. Is. 65:17 _____

5. Read Isaiah 6:1-9. How would you say Isaiah is a disciple?

_____

6. Read Isaiah 40:1-5. How is he a prophet?

_____

"Old Testament Disciples"

An Overview of the Major and Minor Prophets

Session 2: Jeremiah, Prophet to the Nations

+ + +

THE PROPHET

Jeremiah (*"God exalts"*) was from Anathoth, a village 5 miles north of Jerusalem. He was called to be a prophet to Judah and Israel, as well as Babylon. His timidity and knowledge of the disasters to come resulted in his being called "Prophet of Doom" and "Weeping Prophet."

Jeremiah's word of judgment from the Lord made him unpopular among his people. He had only a few friends and found speaking God's Word difficult. He himself wrote nothing. but his loyal secretary, Baruch, recorded all his prophetic words from God.

Called to serve by the Lord at a young age (See 1:4-10), his ministry began around 626 BC and ended 40 years later with his death in 586 BC. His message made him vilified by the people and hated by Kings of Judah and Israel who often placed him under arrest to quiet him.

Jeremiah's life as a prophet was difficult. At various times he was thrown into a cistern, beaten, placed in stocks and imprisoned, all by his fellow Hebrews. Ironically, it was Babylonian King Nebuchadnezzar who freed him and treated him well. King Josiah of Israel was also said to have treated him well, but it was not long lasting, as tradition says Jeremiah was killed by his fellow Judeans. It took courage to be a prophet of God!

THE BOOK

The book of Jeremiah contains more words than any other book, making it the longest book of the Bible. His were mostly words of sadness and condemnation due to the people's sins.

Themes in Jeremiah's book:
1. Judgment, but repentance would avert disaster.
2. God reigns over Judah and all the nations.
3. People are accountable to God for their sins.
4. Destruction is coming due to their evil leaders.
5. God's mercy will triumph. Evil will be defeated.
6. Beware of false prophets, for they, too, are evil.

After the people of Judah were defeated and led into exile in Babylon, Jeremiah spoke God's word that the people should accept their new life without rebellion. God said He would be with them in their new land and they should live life as usual until they could return home.

This message is the reason he wrote the words of 29:11, **For I know the plans I have for you,"** **declares the LORD, "plans to prosper you and not** **to harm you, plans to give you hope and a** **future."** People today often mistake these words as being a gentle reminder of how good life will be for them if they follow the Lord.

But these words were spoken to enslaved people in exile. Thus, his message of *"Submit, don't rebel!"* got him branded as a traitor, and after the exiles returned, Jeremiah was stoned to death. It is from the nation of Judah that the people became known as "Jews." Being a prophet to the Jews required great faith, courage and trust in God.

1. Read these passages from Jeremiah and answer:

a. Jeremiah 1:4-10. What are these verses called?

_____

b. Jeremiah 1:13-14. Who does the "pot" represent?

_____

c. Jeremiah 2:11-13. What do the cisterns symbolize?

_____

d. Jeremiah 9:10. What other book did Jeremiah have written?

_____

e. Jeremiah 18:1-6. What image does he use?

_____

f. Jeremiah 21:1-2. What was Jeremiah told to do?

_____

g. Jeremiah 23:1-4. What is God saying here?

_____

h. Jeremiah 26:7-9. Why was Jeremiah in danger?

_____

i. Jeremiah 29:10-13. What does God promise?

_____

j. Jeremiah 31:15. Where have you read this before?

_____

k. Jeremiah 31:31-34. What does God promise?

_____

l. Jeremiah 32:36-41. What happened in 1947 that caused many people to believe this was God's fulfillment of His promise?

_____

m. Jeremiah 52:12-30. What finally happened?

_____

LAMENTATIONS

This five-chapter book of Hebrew poetry is Jeremiah's lament over what happened to his rebellious fellow Jews. His words may seem silly or unwise in today's era when people emphasize joy, prosperity and self-esteem. Yet they offer an honest look at human sin and guilt, as well as God's steadfast love for those who trust Him.

A modern disciple will learn from the message of Jeremiah in Lamentations. He is truly saddened by what the people have become, yet he does not despair. While there is much to mourn because of sin and evil in life, God's mercy and love is great enough to prevail in this sinful world.

"Old Testament Disciples"

An Overview of the Major and Minor Prophets

Session 3: Ezekiel, Prophet in Exile

+ + +

THE PROPHET

Ezekiel (*"God will strengthen"*) was born in 622 BC, also at Anathoth, into a family of priests. His father was Buzi and Jewish tradition says he was a descendant of Salmon by Rahab. This is doubtful for it would have placed him in the royal line of King David, which Ezekiel surely would have mentioned in his writings.

Jehoiachin, king of Judah, was deposed by the Babylonians in 597 BC, the year Ezekiel was 25 years old and had just been married. At age 30, he was called to be a prophet and lived with his wife by a river near modern-day Tel Aviv. She died four years later, and they had no children. After his wife's death, Ezekiel moved to Jerusalem where Jeremiah was living.

Ezekiel began prophesying incessantly about the destruction of Jerusalem which was fulfilled six years later when the city was sacked and Solomon's glorious Temple was destroyed by the Babylonians in 587 BC.

Ezekiel was among the thousands of upper class and skilled Jews who were exiled to Babylon. At age 50 he began to have visions of the building of a new Temple. He continued to prophesy for 22 years during which time he wrote that he had an encounter with God. He died in exile at around 570 BC.

THE BOOK

The book of Ezekiel is somewhat difficult to understand due to its record of his many visions. To avoid misinterpretation, Jewish tradition required the first and last chapters of Ezekiel not be read by Jewish men before they were 30 years old. The Hebrew text of the book was difficult to understand when it was first written, and today is equally difficult to translate. Some of this may be due to Ezekiel's visions and the rapid way he recorded what he saw.

Like Jeremiah, Ezekiel has favorite expressions which appear throughout his book: *"son of man," "abomination," "Declares the Lord God,"* and others. Ezekiel's writing also includes repeated features of his visions, such as the wheels in the air and the measurements of the new Temple.

Ezekiel communicated God's Word through actions which symbolized things to come. He also includes shocking descriptions of lust and adulterous behaviors, which serve to illustrate the extreme unfaithfulness of Israel and Judah.

A portion of Ezekiel is also devoted to prophesying against nations other than Israel and Judah. This is not so much prejudice against other non-Jewish peoples as it is showing God's rule and judgment over all peoples of the earth. God desires the salvation of all people, not their destruction.

THEMES of EZEKIEL

1. Death and God's wrath comes by the sword, but God keeps His covenant with His people.

2. Israel has not walked according to God's laws, but God will one day renew their hearts.

3. God withdraws His glory and blessings from His unfaithful people, but He will restore their fortunes.

4. The people's idolatry is spiritual adultery and will result in their exile, famine and pestilence. But God will one day give them back their homeland and a new Temple.

5. Tell what each of these passages is about.

a. Ezekiel 2:1-7

_____

b. Ezekiel 3:1-4

_____

c. Ezekiel 3:16-19

_____

d. Ezekiel 11:19-20

_____

e. Ezekiel 18:21-23, 32

_____

f. Ezekiel 34:20-24

_____

6. What are these visions that Ezekiel sees?

a. Ezekiel 1:4-6

_____

b. Ezekiel 8:2-4

_____

c. Ezekiel 37:1-14

_____

d. Ezekiel 40:1-4

_____

e. Ezekiel 43:2-5

_____

7. Old Testament prophets generally had three roles:

a) Preachers who denounced sin and called for repentance.

b) Predictors who announced the coming judgment of God.

c) Watchmen who warned people against falling away from God.

8. Which of those three prophetic roles does Ezekiel fulfill in the following passages?

a. Ezekiel 3:16-17 _____

b. Ezekiel 7:8-9 _____

c. Ezekiel 14:6 _____

9. How did the prophet show he was a disciple in Ezekiel 1:28?

_____

"Old Testament Disciples"
An Overview of the Major and Minor Prophets

<u>Session 4: Daniel, Prophet to Kings</u>

+ + +

THE PROPHET and THE BOOK

Daniel (*"God is my judge"*) was one of the 3,000 skilled Jews removed from Judah to live in Babylon. Details of this exile are recorded in 2 Kings 24 and 2 Chronicles 36. Young Daniel lived from 605 to 536 BC.

He and his young friends were educated in Babylon but never converted to its pagan ways. Daniel is well known for his prophesies and visions about the "Four Monarchies" as recorded in Daniel chapters 2, 7, 10 and 11. His most well-known stories were about the three men in the fiery furnace, the handwriting on the wall, and his experience in the lion's den.

When Neduchadnezzar experienced troubling dreams, the king's "wise men" were unable to tell what they meant, so Daniel was brought to interpret them. The King marveled at the young man's wisdom, declared Daniel's God was *"God of all gods"* and made Daniel governor over the whole country of Babylon. Daniel's friends were also promoted to be with him. Parts of Daniel's story loosely parallel that of Joseph.

The book of Daniel shows the young man's faithfulness, and records some mysterious stories. The entire prophetic book shows how God blesses those who remain faithful to Him when all others around turn away from Him.

1. Which monarchies are listed in these verses?

a. Daniel 2:1

_____

b. Daniel 7:1

_____

c. Daniel 10:1

_____

d. Daniel 11:1

_____

2. What happened to King Nebuchadnezzar in Daniel 4:33?

_____

3. Who is quoted extensively in Daniel 4:34-37? Why?

_____

4. What stories here are usually learned in Sunday School?

a. Daniel 3:12 ff.

_____

b. Daniel 5:13-31

_____

c. Daniel 6:16-24

_____

5. Tell of the visions Daniel experienced in these verses:

a. Daniel 7:1-8 – the vision?

_____

_____

b. Who interpreted this vision for Daniel?

_____

c. Daniel 8:1-14 – the vision?

_____

_____

d. Who interpreted this vision for Daniel?

_____

e. Daniel 10:4-9 – the vision?

_____

_____

6. Daniel is considered by some scholars to be the first book that deals with the End Times. Although Daniel 12 is one of the shorter chapters in this prophetic book, it contains several prophetic scenes that are puzzling and interesting.

a. Daniel 12:1-4 – Who is speaking in this section?

_____

b. What does the man ask in 12:6?

_____

c. What answer is given in 12:7?

_____

d. What does Daniel ask in 12:8?

_____

e. What answer does he receive in 12:9?

_____

f. How would you say Daniel was a disciple of God?

_____

LUTHER ON DANIEL

"From this book of Daniel we see what a splendid, great man Daniel was in the sight of both God and the world. In the sight of God, he above all other prophets had this special prophesy to give. He not only prophesies of Christ, like the others, but also reckons, determines and fixes with certainty the times and years. He also arranges the kingdoms with their doings so precisely and well, in the right succession down to the fixed time of Christ, that one cannot miss the coming of Christ unless one does it willfully. In the sight of the world, too, Daniel was a splendid and great man, ruling kingdoms as their chief prefect." (Preface to the Prophet Daniel)

ADDITIONAL THOUGHT

Babylon may have held Judah captive, but it, too, was also accountable to the Lord. All earthly kingdoms are given their time by God. As Job earlier said, *"The Lord gives and the Lord takes away. Blessed be the name of the Lord."*(Job 1:21)

"Old Testament Disciples"
An Overview of the Major and Minor Prophets

<u>Session 5: Hosea, Prophet of God</u>

+ + +

THE PROPHET

Hosea is the first of the Old Testament Minor Prophets. He was the son of an unknown prophet named Beeri and lived in the 8th century BC, prophesying in the northern kingdom of Israel some 30 years. His name means *"God saves"* and symbolizes His relationship with Israel.

Hosea was a contemporary of Isaiah, Amos and Micah. He lived during the final days of the Northern Kingdom of Israel, just before they were carried off into captivity by Assyria and never returned. At that time, Judah was also exiled into Babylon, but unlike the people Israel, the people of Judah did return to their homeland.

At this time, Israel was filled with idolatry, had abandoned God and His commands, and was spiritually and morally bankrupt. They worshiped at pagan shrines and adopted pagan deities, practicing ritual prostitution and human sacrifice. This led Hosea and other prophets to use prostitution as a "word picture" of the people's unfaithfulness to the Lord.

Hosea vigorously preached against the idolatry of Israel and bravely rebuked the people, as well as its kings and priests, in an attempt to remind them all of the Lord's faithfulness and thus recall them back to God in repentance. They did not heed his call.

17

Hosea was called by God to live, marry and have children with names and activities that symbolized his prophetic message from God. The wife he chose was Gomer, a prostitute, and his children were given names that showed God's faithfulness to unfaithful people.

THE BOOK

With 14 chapters, the book of Hosea is one of the longer of the Minor Prophets. Much of the book takes place during the reign of Jeroboam II of Israel in the north at the same time as Isaiah and Amos were prophesying to Judah in the south.

Despite Jeroboam's success as a king, he persisted in the old idolatry of his ancestor kings of Israel. With their economic prosperity, Hebrew kings led the people in unrighteous living that was an abomination to God.

The book is a severe warning against idolatry and a dramatic call to repentance. Christians draw upon the analogy of Hosea's taking his adulterous wife back into his home as signifying Christ's redemption of all people on the cross. Despite the severity of judgment in Hosea, God's love for His people comes through again and again, as Hosea 1:7 states, *"I will have mercy on the house of Judah and will save them by the Lord their God."*

1. Hosea's Family:

a. Hosea 1:2-3. What was his wife's name and what was she like?

b. Hosea 1:4. What was the name of his son? Why name him this?

_____

c. Hosea 1: 6-7. What was his daughter's name? Why?

_____

d. Hosea 1: 8-9. What was his second son's name? Why?

_____

2. What did Hosea do in chapter 3?

_____

_____

3. What does God do in 4:6-7?

_____

4. How do Israel and Judah seem to respond in 6:1?

_____

5. How does 6:7 show they are not serious in their repentance?

_____

6. What was God's response in 9:1-3?

_____

7. How does God show He still loves His people in 11:1?

_____

8. Where have you heard that passage in the New Testament?

_____

9. What does God say of Himself in 13:4?

_____

10. What does God say to Israel in 14:1-2?

_____

11. How can God still love His people when they continually rebel against Him and fail to do what He requires?

_____

12. How does Hosea show he is a dedicated disciple of the Almighty God in his book?

_____

_____

13. What can we learn about our nation and culture from reading Hosea and seeing his example?

_____

_____

14. What can we learn from Hosea for our personal life?

_____

_____

LUTHER ON HOSEA

"It was common for all the prophets to be doing some strange things as a sign to the people. So Hosea's wife and children had names of harlotry as a sign against the whoring, idolatrous nation." (<u>Lectures on Hosea</u>)

"Old Testament Disciples"
An Overview of the Major and Minor Prophets

Session 6: Joel, Gentle Prophet

+ + +

THE PROPHET

His name means *"the Lord is God"* and he was the son of an unknown man named Pethuel (Joel 1:1). This is all we know for certain about the prophet called Joel.

Because of the content of his book, we can assume he worked in Judah, the southern kingdom, perhaps in Jerusalem. Because this book has traditionally been placed between Hosea and Amos, some are led to think they were contemporaries.

With so little known of him, scholars disagree on the date the book of Joel, placing it during a 400 year period between 800 BC and 400 BC. Because Joel talks about priests but not about a king, some think he may have written his book at the time of priestly leadership at the beginning of the reign of Joash, the boy-king, 835-796 BC. Others say it should be dated after the reign of King Jehoshaphat (3:2) around 873-848 BC or earlier.

Tradition says he was buried at Gush Halav, a town that still exists today in northern Galilee near the slopes of Mt. Hermon.

Joel's statement in 2:28-29, *"I will pour out my spirit upon all flesh; and your sons and your daughters shall prophesy, your old men shall dream dreams, your young men shall see visions,"* was recalled by Peter in his sermon on Pentecost day (Acts 2:17-18).

21

THE BOOK

This prophetic book begins with an invasion of locusts (1:2-4) that is symbolic of the catastrophe that is coming that will strip the land of its wealth and prosperity. This may be a literal plague or is symbolic of the coming invading armies of the Assyrians or Babylonians. Since no other nations are mentioned in Joel, this prophesy is probably not an actual locust plague, but a word picture of God's coming judgment.

Readers of Joel should carefully consider his call to repentance as it applies personally to each person. His comments about the "Day of the Lord" should be taken in all earnestness. Although God is coming to judge the world and to condemn the unrepentant, He is also coming to declare "not guilty" all who trust in His mercy through the Lord Jesus Christ.

LUTHER ON JOEL

"Joel was a kindly and gentle man. He does not denounce and rebuke as do other prophets, but pleads and laments with kind and friendly words to make the people righteous and protect them from harm and misfortune. But as happened with other prophets, the people did not believe his words and held him to be a fool. Nevertheless Joel is highly praise in the New Testament by St. Peter. St. Paul also makes glorious use of the saying, 'Everyone who calls upon the name of the Lord will be saved' (Joel 2:32). In the first chapter Joel prophesies of the punishment which is to come upon the people of Israel. In the second place he prophesies of the Kingdom of Christ and of the Holy Spirit."
(Lectures on Joel)

1. Joel 1:5. Why will drunkards weep?

_____

2. Joel 1:11. Why should "tillers of the soil" be ashamed?

_____

3. What are the people called to do in 1:13?

_____

4. What is coming in 2:1? What should someone do?

_____

5. How is the "day of the Lord" described in 2:2a?

_____

6. What appears to be coming in 2:2b-5?

_____

7. What does Joel call the people to do in 2:12-13?

_____

8. What might God decide to do in 2:14?

_____

9. What does 2:18 tell us happened?

_____

10. What does God promise in 2:24-26?

_____

11. What will they know as a result of God's mercy (verse27)?

_____

12. Joel 2:28-29 is quoted by Peter on Pentecost. How do you think Peter could do such a thing in his mighty sermon?

_____

13. What will happen on the great "day of the Lord" (verse 30-31)

_____

14. St. Paul quoted the words of Joel 2:32 in Romans 10:13. Look up that passage. What other Old Testament prophet does Paul quote in Romans 10:11 and 10: 15?

_____

15. What does Joel urge them to do in 3:10?

_____

16. Where in Isaiah is the same image?_____

16. Discuss: Would errant Christians today respond better to the message of a Prophet Joel or a Prophet Hosea? Why do you think so?

_____

_____

_____

"Old Testament Disciples"
An Overview of the Major and Minor Prophets

<u>Session 7: Amos, Shepherd Prophet</u>

+ + +

THE PROPHET and his TIMES

The Lord called this prophet to deliver a surprising and ominous message for the people of both Israel and Judah. He lived and did his work in the southern kingdom, during the reign of King Uzziah, also known as Azariah, in 792-740 BC. The history of this time period is found in 2 Kings 14-15 and 2 Chronicles 26.

Amos was a shepherd from Tekoa, 6 miles south of Bethlehem and 12 miles from Jerusalem. Amos' name means *"burden bearer,"* and he also cared for sycamore fig trees. While tending his flocks, God called him to take a message to Israel, now ruled by King Jeroboam II (793-753 BC). We don't hear of Amos in any other part of the Bible except in this book.

It was a time when Judah was expanding, restoring its borders to former size. It was a time of great idolatry, extravagant living, immorality, corruption by judicial procedures and oppression of the poor. The Assyrians would invade and capture Israel in 722 BC.

Tragically, the people were following in the steps of King Jeroboam I, the founder of the northern kingdom. The books of Kings and Chronicles are filled with examples how the rulers *"followed in the sins of Jeroboam, son of Nebat, which he had caused Israel to commit."*

The sins of Judah occurred at a time of military victories, expanded territories and renewed national pride. Despite such blessings, Israel succumbed to their terrible sins, falling further and further away from the Lord.

The message Amos took them would be difficult to deliver. Times were great and they didn't want to hear him. He also warned the southern kingdom of Judah, as we see references to Judah and Jerusalem in his words.

THE BOOK

Amos' key message was that God, the Great King who rules the whole universe, will judge his unfaithful, disobedient, covenant-breaking people, and it will be disastrous for them unless they repent. Amos pictures the Lord as an angry, crouching lion stalking the sinful, carefree nations. Amos' unpopular prophecies of destruction were rapidly fulfilled by the invading Assyrians who began by besieging Samaria, which lay between Israel and Judah.

LUTHER ON AMOS

"Amos lived and preached in the days of Hosea and Isaiah. He attacks the same vices, idolatry and false sanctity as does Hosea and forewarns of the coming Assyrian captivity. He violently denounces the people of Israel through almost the entire book until the end of the last chapter where he prophesies of Christ and His kingdom, and closes his book with that. No prophet, I think, has so little in the way of promises and so much in the way of denunciations." (Lectures on Amos)

1. Amos 1:1, Where was the author from?

_____

2. The text moves in a circle, pronouncing judgment on the nations around before finally taking aim at Judah and then at Israel. What places are mentioned in:

a. Amos 1:3?

_____

b. Amos 1:6?

_____

c. Amos 1:11?

_____

d. Amos 1:13?

_____

e. Amos 2:1?

_____

3. Amos 2:4. Who does the prophet address? _____

a. What is their sin that he condemns?

_____

b. What will God send upon them?

_____

4. Amos 2:6. What other country is named? _____

a. What is their sin that he condemns?

_____

b. What will God send upon them?

_____

5. What vision in chapter 7 is similar to Joel's vision?

_____

6. What image is given in Amos 7:7?

_____

7. Of what is Amos accused in 7:12?

_____

8. What does the basket of summer fruit symbolize in 8:1-3?

_____

9. What does God say He will do in 9:11?

_____

10. What is God describing in Amos 9:13-14?

_____

11. What does He promise them in 9:15?

_____

12. How did Amos show himself a disciple of God?

_____

"Old Testament Disciples"

An Overview of the Major and Minor Prophets

Session 8: Obadiah, Prophet to Edom

+ + +

A ONE-CHAPTER BOOK

¹ *The vision of Obadiah. Thus says the Lord God concerning Edom: We have heard a report from the Lord, and a messenger has been sent among the nations: "Rise up! Let us rise against her for battle!"* ² *Behold, I will make you small among the nations; you shall be utterly despised.* ³ *The pride of your heart has deceived you, you who live in the clefts of the rock, in your lofty dwelling, who say in your heart, "Who will bring me down to the ground?"* ⁴ *Though you soar aloft like the eagle, though your nest is set among the stars, from there I will bring you down, declares the Lord.* ⁵ *If thieves came to you, if plunderers came by night — how you have been destroyed! — would they not steal only enough for themselves? If grape gatherers came to you, would they not leave gleanings?* ⁶ *How Esau has been pillaged, his treasures sought out!* ⁷ *All your allies have driven you to your border; those at peace with you have deceived you; they have prevailed against you; those who eat your bread have set a trap beneath you — you have no understanding.* ⁸ *Will I not on that day, declares the Lord, destroy the wise men out of Edom, and understanding out of Mount Esau?* ⁹ *And your mighty men shall be dismayed, O Teman, so that every man from Mount Esau will be cut off by slaughter.* ¹⁰ *Because of the violence done to your brother Jacob, shame shall cover you, and you shall be cut off forever.* ¹¹ *On the day that you stood aloof, on the day that strangers carried off his wealth and foreigners entered his gates and cast lots for Jerusalem, you were like one of them.* ¹² *But do not gloat over the day of your brother in the day of his misfortune; do not rejoice over the people of Judah in the day of their ruin; do not boast in the day of*

distress. ¹³ Do not enter the gate of my people in the day of their calamity; do not gloat over his disaster in the day of his calamity; do not loot his wealth in the day of his calamity. ¹⁴ Do not stand at the crossroads to cut off his fugitives; do not hand over his survivors in the day of distress. ¹⁵ For the day of the Lord is near upon all the nations. As you have done, it shall be done to you; your deeds shall return on your own head. ¹⁶ For as you have drunk on my holy mountain, so all the nations shall drink continually; they shall drink and swallow, and shall be as though they had never been. ¹⁷ But in Mount Zion there shall be those who escape, and it shall be holy, and the house of Jacob shall possess their own possessions. ¹⁸ The house of Jacob shall be a fire, and the house of Joseph a flame, and the house of Esau stubble; they shall burn them and consume them, and there shall be no survivor for the house of Esau, for the Lord has spoken.¹⁹ Those of the Negeb shall possess Mount Esau, and those of the Shephelah shall possess the land of the Philistines; they shall possess the land of Ephraim and the land of Samaria, and Benjamin shall possess Gilead. ²⁰ The exiles of this host of the people of Israel shall possess the land of the Canaanites as far as Zarephath, and the exiles of Jerusalem who are in Sepharad shall possess the cities of the Negeb. ²¹ Saviors shall go up to Mount Zion to rule Mount Esau, and the kingdom shall be the Lord's.

+ + +

HISTORY OF EDOM

The majority of the people of Edom were descendants of Esau, twin brother of Jacob, who had separated from him before going to Egypt at the invitation of Jacob's son Joseph. After the conquest of the Promised Land, King Saul defeated the Edomites and made them vassals.

The Edomites lived in the southern desert area of Judah called the Negeb (wilderness) where they were ruled by Jewish governors which David put in place. After the division of Israel and Judah, Edom was controlled by Judah. When Judah was defeated by Nebuchadnezzar in 586, Edom joined forces against their distant cousins who had controlled them.

After the Babylonian deportation, the Edomites moved into southern Judah and set up their capital in Hebron which they renamed Idumaea. They intermarried with some of the Jewish remnant not taken into exile.

Later, during the Maccabean revolt in 164 BC, Edomites were forcibly converted to Judaism. One of their leaders, Antipater, a man of mixed Jewish-Edomite blood, was appointed governor by the Romans in 63 BC, and his son, Herod, founded the dynasty of kings that dominated Israel during the New Testament times.

THE BOOK

1. The book was written after 586 BC when Judah and Israel had been defeated by its enemies. Obadiah's name means *"servant of God."* Whom does he prophesy against (verse 8)?

_____

2. Why is God angry against them (verse 11-12)?

_____

3. As a result of Edom's lack of compassion, what will happen?

_____

4. What people lived in the country of Edom? (see verse 8)

_____

5. How were the Edomites related to Israel and Judah?

_____

6. What seems to be the source of God's wrath in verse 3 and 12?

_____

7. What is meant by *"the House of Jacob"* in verses 17-18?

_____

8. Why would that term be meaningful in Edomite history?

_____

9. What irony do you see in Herod being appointed governor over Edom after Judah's early history with the Edomites?

_____

_____

10. Read Revelation 11:15. This echoes verse 21. Where have you heard these words before?

_____

11. Martin Luther saw a prophesy of Christ's kingdom in Obadiah 20-21. God mixes all the nations together as Lord of all the peoples. How does this apply to Jesus?

_____

"Old Testament Disciples"

An Overview of the Major and Minor Prophets

<u>Session 9: Jonah, Reluctant Prophet</u>

+ + +

THE PROPHET

Jonah was a prophet from Israel, son of Amittai a prophet from Gath Hepher, a village near Nazareth. He is not mentioned as the author of his book, so it was probably written by someone else. The meaning of his name is unknown.

Besides this book, Jonah is referenced only one other time in the Old Testament, in 2 Kings 14:25 when King Jeroboam II restored the borders of Israel *"...according to the word of the L*ORD*, the God of Israel, which he spoke by his servant Jonah."*

Jonah was mentioned in the New Testament by Jesus three times, Matthew chapters 12 and 16 and Luke 11, each time when Jesus spoke of showing His critics *"the sign of Jonah."* This referred to his 3 days buried inside the fish which corresponded to Jesus' 3 days in the tomb.

Jonah was a Galilean prophet, the first sent to preach specifically to the Gentiles. He prophesied during the reign of Jeroboam II, 793-753 BC and was a contemporary of Amos, Hosea, and Micah.

This was a time of spiritual poverty in Israel under an evil king, a time of captivity by the Assyrians. In 722 BC this savage nation defeated Israel and took them into exile. As Assyria conquered more and more land, Israel neglected the affairs at home and was in great turmoil.

LUTHER ON JONAH

"As Jerome (347-420 AD) claimed, some believe Jonah was the son of the widow of Zarapheth near Sidon who fed Elijah during the famine (1 Kings 17:8-24 and Luke 4:26). The reason given is that Jonah calls himself the son of Amittai, ("True One") because the widow told Elijah after he raised her son from death, said, "Now I know the word of your mouth is true." (1 Kings 17:24) Let anyone believe this who wants. I do not believe it."

THE BOOK

Critical scholars claim the story of Jonah is a fictional account of a man being miraculously rescued by God through a fish. However, all other aspects of the story conform to the historical setting. Nineveh was the capital of Assyria, one of the oldest cities in the world, founded by Nimrod, the great-grandson of Noah shortly after the Flood. (Genesis 10:9-12)

Jesus' reference to *"the sign of Jonah"* includes more than time spent inside the fish. He also meant He would soon be under both His Father's judgment and His Father's salvation.

Other parallels between Jonah and Jesus include: (1) Jonah's descent into Sheol and Christ's descent to hell, (2) Christ's crying out on the cross in abandonment and Jonah's prayer to God from inside the fish, and (3) Jesus and Jonah both experiencing judgment, condemnation and death before they experienced new life.

1. Read Jonah chapter 1:

a. Why did Jonah run away from God?

b. What did God use to thwart his plans to escape on a ship?

_____

c. Why were the sailors fearful?

_____

d. Where did the captain find Jonah?

_____

e. What did he want Jonah to do?

_____

f. Why did the sailors decide to toss Jonah overboard?

_____

2. Read Jonah chapter 2:

a. What did Jonah pray from inside the fish?

_____

b. What did the fish do?

_____

3. Read Jonah chapter 3:

a. What message was Jonah told to tell Nineveh?

_____

b. How did the people react to his message?

_____

4. Read Jonah chapter 4:

a. How did Jonah react to the Nineveh's repentance?

_____

b. Why do you think he reacted this way?

_____

c. What was God trying to show Jonah in the plant?

_____

d. What made Jonah angry?

_____

e. What did God ask Jonah?

_____

f. What do you think is meant in 4:11 by *"persons who do not know their right hand from their left"?*

_____

g. What do you think is the real reason Jonah was angry?

_____

h. Does a disciple have reason to get angry? Why?

_____

i. How do you think Jonah showed himself to be a disciple?

_____

_____

"Old Testament Disciples"

An Overview of the Major and Minor Prophets

Session 10: Micah, Prophet to Judah
+ + +

THE PROPHET

Micah was from Moresheth, an insignificant village in Judah 25 miles southwest of Jerusalem. His name means, *"Who is like God?"* He preached during Kings Jotham, Ahaz and Hezekiah.

In Judah this was a time of political instability, social injustice, moral degeneracy and spiritual poverty. Idolatry was wide-spread and worship of God had become a mere formality, with the people going through the motions, but their hearts were not in it.

Judah had been invaded by Israel, so King Ahaz had appealed to Assyria for protection. Thus Judah had given up their independence and annually was forced to pay huge amounts to Assyria for their protection.

Micah was a contemporary of Hosea and Isaiah. He preached God's Word in the southern kingdom from 737 until 696 B.C. when Assyria defeated the northern kingdom of Israel.

LUTHER ON MICAH

"Micah lived at the time of Isaiah. He even uses the words of Isaiah 2:2-4 which shows they were contemporaries. Micah one of the fine prophets who rebukes the people severely for their idolatry and constantly refers to the coming Christ and His kingdom. He is unique among

37

prophets in that he points with certainty to Bethlehem as the town where Christ was to be born. Matthew shows this in Matthew 2:3-6 (Lectures on Micah)

THE BOOK

Micah prophesied the future destruction of Jerusalem and Samaria but also the future restoration of the Judean state. He rebuked the people of Judah for their dishonesty and idolatry. He preached against the wealthy leaders of Judah and Israel who indulged themselves. Despite his message, they did not see the dangers around them, including the threat of exile.

When Micah made his predictions, he said the city was doomed because its beautification was financed by dishonest business practices and impoverished the citizens. He also condemned the prophets of his day for accepting money for telling dishonest oracles.

Besides the destruction of Judah, Micah also predicted its restoration as being more glorious than before. He prophesied an era of universal peace over which the Governor will rule from Jerusalem. He declared that when the glory of Zion and Jacob is restored, the Lord will force the Gentiles to abandon their idolatry.

Micah also prophesied the coming of a faithful Shepherd who would stand guard over His people and defend them like a lion. This new Shepherd Ruler would come from the shepherd's town, Bethlehem, and would go to the City of David from where he would renew the kingdom. Micah's Shepherd is, of course, Jesus of Nazareth.

1. Read Micah 1:3-8

a. How does Micah begin his book?

_____

b. Where is Samaria (verse 6)?

_____

c. What are the "carved images" in verse 7?

_____

d. Why do you think "Her wound is incurable" (1:9)?

_____

2. Read Micah 4:1-5 (See also Isaiah 2:2-4)

a. What do you think is meant by *"the mountain of the House of the Lord"* (verse 1)?

_____

b. What is another word for *"nations"* (verse 2)?

_____

c. Where have you heard verse 3b before? (See Isaiah 11:6)

_____

d. Why do you think this concept is repeated often in the Bible?

_____

e. Who do you think is meant by *"peoples"* in verse 5?

_____

3. Read Micah 5:1-6

a. When is 5:2 heard most often?

_____

b. Who is the shepherd of his flock in verse 4?

_____

c. In verse 5, why is Assyria mentioned?

_____

4. Read Micah 6:8. What three things does God require of us?

a. _____

b. _____

c. _____

5. Read Micah 7:5-8

a. What instruction is given in verses 5-6? Why?

_____

b. Who is the only trustworthy person (verse 7)?

_____

6. Read Micah 7:18-20. Name four things will God do for us.

a. _____

b. _____

c. _____

d. _____

"Old Testament Disciples"
An Overview of the Major and Minor Prophets

Session 11: Nahum, Prophet to Nineveh

+ + +

THE PROPHET

We know little about Nahum except what he tells us in 1:1, his name (a common one) and that he is from Elkosh. We don't know where this city was but most scholars place it somewhere in Judah. We do know his name means *"comfort."*

Beginning in 663 BC, Nahum prophesied against the people of Nineveh, both to warn them of the coming disaster and to give hope to the people of Judah who were under Nineveh's rule. Jonah had prophesied against this city a hundred years before resulting in their repentance.

Nahum's message was not so well received. The city was at its peak of glory and the only superpower of its time, so his message was shrugged off as unbelievable. As a result, Nineveh was sacked by a coalition of armies in 612 BC.

The northern kingdom of Israel had already been captured by Assyria at this time, and his message of destruction for Nineveh, Assyria's capital, was meant to give comfort and hope to the captive people of Judah as the time was coming when they would see how God is in control.

Nineveh was very old and huge, at 30 miles long and 10 miles wide, with 120,000 people. Built by the Tigris River, it was a wealthy metropolis built by slave labor and plunder from neighboring countries during their vicious battles.

Capernaum was the fishing village on the north side of the Sea of Galilee, known for its connection to Jesus' ministry and His disciples. Its name means *"village of Nahum."* Despite the similarity, there appears to be no connection between the village and this prophet.

THE BOOK

Like the other prophets, Nahum begins by being God's mouthpiece in an oracle of judgment (1:1). Nahum first speaks of God's wrath against ungodliness everywhere, but then moves on to accuse Nineveh specifically.

Nahum uses imaginative word pictures in this brief book of 3 chapters. His words of judgment, though used sparingly, strike like a hammer against Nineveh's ungodliness. God's mercy towards the people a hundred years before had long run out. They now faced the full wrath of His judgment.

In an unusual change of pattern, God does not deliver to them a final word of grace and mercy. As He says in Nahum 3:19, *"There is no easing your hurt; your wound is grievous."*

1. Read Nahum chapter one. List 4 characteristics of God as listed in verses 1-11:

a. _____

b. _____

c. _____

d. _____

2. Do any of these characteristics surprise you?

_____

3. Judah and Nineveh both had sinned greatly. Why do you think God is being harder on Nineveh than on Judah?

_____

_____

4. Read Nahum chapter 2. The prophet describes the fall of Nineveh with brilliant pictures of the frantic activity as they are being attacked by the Medes and Babylonians, who often dressed their warriors in red. The troops are moving so quickly they stumble over each other. Nineveh had built a great dam to store up water in the rainy season for use in the dry season. Most of the city's buildings were made of mud brick.

a. How did their enemies defeat Nineveh (2:3-8)?

_____

b. What did its enemies do in 2:9?

_____

c. How are its people described in 2:10?

_____

d. What is Assyria's symbol of power (2:11)? What happened to it?

_____

e. What does God say He will do to them in 2:13?

_____

5. Read Nahum chapter 3. Thebes, situated on the Nile, was the capital of ancient Egypt and home of the Pharaohs. It was a world class power and its neighbors, Cush, Libya and Putt, were aligned with it. But their pride in their strategic position and military power did not stop Assyria from conquering it in 663 B.C. Nahum says Nineveh should have learned from Thebes.

a. To what does Nahum compare Assyria in 3:4-8?

_____

b. Doesn't it seem ironic that a man whose name meant "comfort" wrote such harsh words? Who is he writing to comfort?

_____

c. How can Nahum's message be relevant to us today?

_____

_____

LUTHER ON NAHUM

"At the end of chapter 1, Nahum talks like Isaiah 52 of the good preachers who proclaim peace and salvation on the mountains, and he bids Judah joyfully to celebrate. Though this can refer to the time of Hezekiah when Judah was rescued and survived, this is a general prophecy referring also to Christ. The destruction of Nineveh is limited so that the righteous remnant was preserved, as Hezekiah and those like him then experienced. Despite the terrible prophecy in Nahum the good news and joyous worship of God, as taught in God's Word, did remain in Judah. In this way the prophet is properly called a true 'Nahum'(comfort)." (Lectures on Nahum)

"Old Testament Disciples"
An Overview of the Major and Minor Prophets

Session 12: <u>Habakkuk, Righteous Prophet</u>

+ + +

THE PROPHET and THE BOOK

Habakkuk is a mysterious prophet. His name appears only twice in this small prophetic book, in Habakkuk 1:1 and 3:1. The pronunciation of his name is even a mystery although the emphasis is placed on the second syllable (ha - BAK - kuk). The name is of Hebrew origin but its meaning is somewhat unclear. Some scholars have connected it to an Akkadian word for a fragrant plant. Martin Luther believes the name it is from the Hebrew verb that means *"to embrace."*

But his message in this brief three chapter book is quite clear. He debates with God, almost arguing with Him as he complains about the lack of justice in Judah (Habakkuk 1:2-4). Like Job, Habakkuk questions why evil exists and why the Lord permits it to afflict His people. But God's answers may not satisfy our human sense of fairness or goodness, since God's ways are higher than our human ways.

Habakkuk had a strong faith and trusted in God implicitly. His name is mentioned in the apocryphal book <u>Bel and the Dragon</u>, an addition to the book of Daniel, where an angel lifted him up by his hair, transported him to Daniel while he was in the lion's den. In the story Habakkuk gave Daniel some food, and then was returned to his home. It's an interesting story, certainly a legend.

We estimate Habakkuk wrote at about the end of the Assyrian empire, just as Babylon was beginning to take power. This makes him a contemporary of Nahum in the northern kingdom, and Zephaniah and Jeremiah in the southern kingdom. Israel had already been taken captive by Assyria, so Habakkuk surely prophesied to the southern kingdom.

Good King Josiah had attempted reforms in the southern kingdom. But after his death his son, King Jehoiakim, brought back all of the godless attitudes and wicked behaviors that we've talked about in previous studies. Habakkuk would have been writing at about that time.

The book of Habakkuk consists of five oracles against the Chaldeans (Babylonians) which rose to power in 612 BC, so scholars usually date the book slightly later, around 605 BC. Habakkuk is unique among the prophets in that he openly questions the working of God (1:3b, 1:13b).

The final chapter 3 is in the form of a song, so some have said Habakkuk might have been from the priestly tribe of Levi which served as musicians in the Temple at that time.

LUTHER ON HABAKKUK

"Habakkuk is a prophet of comfort who is to strengthen and support the people, to prevent them from despairing of the coming Savior. This is why he uses every device and stratagem that can serve to keep strong in their hearts the faith in that promised Christ... Habakkuk's song [chapter 3] says, "In wrath God still remembers mercy." (<u>Lectures on Habakkuk</u>)

1. Read Habakkuk 1: 2-2:5.

a. What appears to be taking place in these verses?

_____

b. What is the topic of Habakkuk 1:2-4?

_____

c. How does God respond in 1:5-11?

_____

d. What is the prophet asking in 1:12?

_____

e. What does the prophet say God does in 1:14?

_____

f. What will happen according to 2:1-2?

_____

g. Where have you heard 2:4? Who found this passage important?

_____

2. Read Habakkuk 2:6-20. What are the Five Woes God speaks to the Chaldeans?

1) _____

2) _____

3) _____

4) _____

5) _____

47

3. Where have you heard the words of 2:20 before?

_____

4. Read Habakkuk 3:1-19. It is a prayer in the form of a song.

a. 3:2 - What has the prophet heard?

_____

b. Teman and Mt. Paran are in Edomite country. What does Habakkuk see there in 3:3-7?

1) _____

2) _____

3) _____

4) _____

5) _____

c. What does 3:10 tell us that creation did during God's wrath?

_____

_____

d. What is the purpose of God's actions in 3:13?

_____

e. What does the prophet say he will do in 3:16b?

_____

f. How does Habakkuk end his song in 3:18-19?

_____

_____

"Old Testament Disciples"

An Overview of the Major and Minor Prophets

Session 13: Zephaniah, Prophet of Change

+ + +

THE PROPHET

Zephaniah's father was Cushi and his Hebrew name means *"God has concealed."* From his genealogy in chapter 1:1, he may have been the great-great-grandson of King Hezekiah, a good king who tried to reform Judah. If this is true the current king, Josiah, also a righteous man, would be a cousin to this prophet.

King Josiah ruled from 640-609 B.C. He was crowned when he was only 8 years old. Initially he was under the influence of advisors who carried on the sins of his father, Amon. But as he became older, Josiah held back from following his advisors in everything and looked for ways to do better than they had done.

While repairing the temple, workers found the Hebrew Book of the Law. King Josiah read it, and with it began some much needed reforms in Jerusalem. Zephaniah may have worked with Josiah to institute these godly changes.

Zephaniah's contemporaries were Nahum, Habakkuk and Jeremiah. Nineveh fell in 612 BC and the rest of Assyria was finally defeated by the Babylonians in 605 B.C. The first Jews, including Daniel, were deported at that time. Zephaniah would have lived during these days.

Zephaniah spoke boldly against the religious and moral corruption of his day. In view of the idolatry which had penetrated even into the sanctuary, he warned that God would "*destroy out of this place the remnant of Baal, and the names of the priests*" (1:4). He pleaded for a return to the simplicity of their fathers' culture instead of the luxurious foreign clothing which was worn, especially in aristocratic circles (1:8).

THE BOOK

Zephaniah prophesied the future storm of God's wrath as a day in complete darkness. Though the world witnessed God's judgment on Judah and its enemies, the prophet's darkest prophecy had remained unfulfilled, the great Day of the Lord which would come at the world's end.

Readers will be challenged to understand the theme of Judgment Day in this prophecy. They can easily feel overwhelmed by descriptions of God's wrath. However, the book ends with a joyful reference to God's mercy in 3:14-20.

LUTHER ON ZEPHANIAH

"In the third chapter, Zephaniah prophesies gloriously and clearly of the happy and blessed kingdom of Christ which shall be spread abroad in all the world. Although he is a minor prophet, he speaks more about Christ than many major prophets, almost even more than Jeremiah. He does so in order to give the people abundant comfort so they would not despair of God because of their disastrous captivity in Babylon, as if God had cut them off forever. Rather he told them they could be sure they would receive His grace again in the promised Savior Christ, with His glorious kingdom."
(Lectures on Zephaniah)

1. Read Zephaniah chapter 1.

a. Who is the prophet's grandfather? Great-grandfather?

_____

b. What word picture does God use to show His wrath in 1:2-3?

_____

c. What is the "remnant of Baal" doing in 1:5-6?

_____

d. What is coming in verse 7?

_____

e. What will God do at that time (1:8-10)?

_____

f. What should the inhabitants do in that day (1:11)?

_____

g. What sounds very near, according to 1:14-15?

_____

h. What cannot deliver them, according to verses 18?

_____

2. Read Zephaniah chapter 2.

a. What does the prophet call the people in verse 1?

_____

b. What does the prophet tell the people to do in verse 3?

_____

c. What words in the verse sound like the meaning of "Zephaniah"?

_____

d. Gaza, Ashkelon, Ashdon and Ekron are all Judah's enemies. "Cherethites" are from the island of Crete which still had some Canaanites living there. What shall happen to them all?

_____

e. "Taunts of Moab" (verse 8) sound like something another prophet warned against. Who was that prophet?

_____

f. What does God say will happen to all Judah's enemies (2:9-15)?

_____

3. Read chapter 3:1-13.

a. On whom is God now pronouncing judgment?

_____

b. What will happen to Judah on the "Day of the Lord" (3:11-12)?

_____

4. Read chapter 3:14-20.

 What great change is seen here from the preceding words of the prophet?

_____

"Old Testament Disciples"

An Overview of the Major and Minor Prophets

<u>Session 14: Haggai, Builder Prophet</u>

+ + +

THE PROPHET

Haggai's name is unique in that it does not refer to a relationship to God as do most Hebrew names. It means *"my holiday"* and is mentioned only in this book and in the book of Ezra 5-6 where Haggai and Zechariah are prophesying to the people of Judah about rebuilding the temple.

The Book of Haggai is unique in that it was written after the Jews returned from their 70 year Babylonian captivity. Until now prophets spoke God's Word to the people before or during their exile. When the first group of people returned from Babylon in 536 B.C, Haggai then prophesied his message to Judah.

From 536-520 BC, the returnees built homes and planted crops to re-establish their lives. Rebuilding of the temple, they decided, could come later. There was also local opposition from those who had not left Judah who feared a new Temple could spark more trouble, even war.

After 16 years the returnees had little to show for their efforts. They had chosen to invest all their efforts in their own homes and lives rather than in their relationship with God. Haggai's message is simple and direct: *"Build God's house!"* He said they must put God's House first and their own needs second. The prophet's words had results - they built the Temple in four years.

This rebuilt temple was finally dedicated in 516 BC. Some scholars believe Haggai may have seen Solomon's temple before it was destroyed, based on 2:3 which says, *"Who among you is left who has seen this house in its former glory?"* If true, this would make the prophet 75-80 years old.

LUTHER ON HAGGAI

"Haggai was the first prophet given to the people after the Babylonian captivity. Zechariah was later given to him as a companion, so that by the mouth of two witnesses the Word of God might be believed more surely. The people had fallen into great doubt whether the Temple would ever be rebuilt. For this reason they were afflicted with famine and loss of produce and crops. This was an example to the godless who paid no heed to God's Word and worship and are always filling their own bags. It is to them that Haggai 1:6 applies the words, 'Their bag shall be full of holes'." (Lectures on Haggai)

THE BOOK

The book of Haggai has a very narrow focus, to rebuild the Temple. The Judeans completed the building just four years after Haggai's brief prophetic work. Readers today may wonder what this prophecy means for them or even why such a specific matter was included in the Bible. It is to show what happens when God is placed first in life. An outline of this brief book is simple:

Chapter 1: Haggai says *"Rebuild!"* and the people obey his command.

Chapter 2: The Temple turns out to be glorious and Zerubbabel is officially chosen their leader.

1. Read Haggai 1:1-15:

a. When did the prophet begin his work?

_____

b. Who is the first man to receive Haggai's words from God?

_____

c. Who also will receive the prophet Haggai's words?

_____

d. What is Haggai's basic message to them in 1:4?

_____

e. What words show they have not prospered yet? (1:6)

_____

f. Where can they get materials for building the Temple (1:7-8)?

_____

g. What is further evidence they had not prospered (1:10-11)?

_____

h. Who responded first to Haggai's prophecy?

_____

i. Why did he have energy and zeal to do the work (verse 14)?

_____

j. When was the work started (verse 15)?

_____

2. Read Haggai 2:1-9:

a. To whom does God tell Haggai to prophesy in 2:2?

    1) _____

    2) _____

    3) _____

b. What is God's command in 2:4?

_____

c. What does God tell them in 2:6-7?

_____

d. How will they have enough money to do the work (verse 8-9)?

_____

3. Read Haggai 2:10-19a.

a. What seems to be the people's past problem?

_____

b. What does God say He will do for them now (verse 2:19b)?

_____

c. What does God do for Zerubbabel (v. 23)?

_____

d. This Bible Study is titled <u>Old Testament Disciples</u>. A "disciple" is one who learns from God. Who are the disciples in this book?

_____

"Old Testament Disciples"

An Overview of the Major and Minor Prophets

Session 15: Zechariah, Comforting Prophet

+ + +

THE PROPHET

Zechariah's name means *"God has remembered,"* and he was called to work with Haggai to encourage the people to obey the Lord. Zechariah is sometimes called the *"Prophet of Holy Week"* since at least three of his prophecies are quoted during that final week of Christ's earthly life.

He was born in Babylonia and returned to Judah in 538 B.C. under the leadership of Zerubbabel and Joshua. He worked with the older prophet Haggai to help rebuild the Jerusalem Temple. Zechariah and Haggai were also contemporaries of the prophet Ezra whose book is between 2 Chronicles and Nehemiah.

Luther calls him one of the more comforting prophets. He was both a prophet (1:1) and a priest, succeeding his grandfather, Iddo, who was also a priest. (Nehemiah 12:10-16)

LUTHER ON ZECHARIAH

"He is truly one of the most comforting of the prophets. He helped Haggai bring the scattered people together again and presents many lovely and reassuring visions, and gives many sweet and kindly words in order to encourage and strengthen the troubled and scattered people to proceed with the Temple building and their government, despite the great and varied resistance which they had encountered."
(Lectures on Zechariah)

THE BOOK

The purpose of Zechariah's book is similar to that of other prophets, to rebuke the people of Judah so they will live according to God's commands. In this case he was to encourage them to complete rebuilding the temple and to bring about a spiritual renewal among all those who had returned from exile, as well as those who had been left behind generations before.

The book begins with 8 visions Zechariah had one night. They are not dreams since he says he had them while being fully awake (4:1). Yet they were surreal and strange, like night dreams.

As you read and answer these questions about Zechariah, try to understand his words for what they said at the time he wrote them. In this way you might also find meaning in them for today.

1. Tell what Zechariah's eight visions were:

a. Zechariah1:7-17

_____

b. Zechariah 1:18-21

_____

c. Zechariah chapter 2

_____

d. Zechariah chapter 3

_____

e. Zechariah 4

_____

f. Zechariah 5:1-4

_____

g. Zechariah 5:5-11

_____

h. Zechariah 6:1-8

_____

2. What happens in Zechariah 6:9-15?

_____

3. Who does Zechariah denounce in 10:1-5? Why?

a. Who? _____

b. Why? _____

4. Here are three readings from Zechariah that speak of things happening to Jesus during Holy Week. Tell what they are and how they related to the events of our Lord during that week.

a. Zechariah 9:9

_____

b. Zechariah 12:10

_____

c. Zechariah 13:7

_____

5. Chapter 14 gives some descriptive pictures of the Last Day. What does each one say?

a. Zechariah 14:1-5

_____

b. Zechariah 14:6-7

_____

c. Zechariah 14:8

_____

d. Zechariah 14:9

_____

e. Zechariah 14:10-15

_____

f. Zechariah 14: 16-19

_____

6. Why is Zechariah 14:20-21 especially comforting?

_____

_____

"Old Testament Disciples"
An Overview of the Major and Minor Prophets

Session 16: Malachi, Preparing Prophet
+ + +
THE PROPHET

Malachi's name means *"my messenger"* and he is the last prophet from God until John the Baptist, about 400 years later.

The Temple had been rebuilt 75-80 years before and more Jews had returned from Babylon, including the priests. Under the leadership of Nehemiah, the walls of Jerusalem had been rebuilt 10-15 years earlier. Ezra had read the Book of the Law at the dedication of the walls and many of the people had committed to changing their ways and following God's commands.

However, a few years later the people became disillusioned with their lives and no longer trusted in God's promises. Their priests had become corrupt and their worship had deteriorated. Most of the people no longer took the Law seriously.

Into this environment, God sent Malachi to reprimand, reassure, and warn God's people.

LUTHER ON MALACHI

"The Hebrews believed Malachi was Ezra. We let that pass because we can know nothing certain about him except that, so far as we can gather from his prophecy, he lived not long before Christ's birth and was certainly the last prophet. Malachi was a fine prophet, and his book contains beautiful sayings about Christ and the Gospel. He calls it 'a pure offering for our world,' for by the Gospel the grace of God is praised and it is the true and pure thank-offering. Malachi

prophesies of the coming of John the Baptist, as Christ Himself in Matthew 10 interprets that of which Malachi writes, calling John His messenger and second Elijah. Beyond this the prophet denounces his people severely because they do not give the priests their tithes and other services. Even when they gave them, they did so faithlessly, giving sick and blemished animals rather than good ones, or whatever they did not want themselves. These had to be good enough for the poor priests and preachers. This is the way it usually goes." (<u>Lectures on the Minor Prophets</u>)

THE BOOK

Malachi's prophesy sought to purify the Levites who were the spiritual leaders of Judah. Their unfaithfulness and impurity is symbolized by their offerings which were left-overs and sick animals instead of the first-fruits. The prophet says that if they do not give God honor in their offerings, He will send a curse upon them (2:2) because their offerings do not come from their hearts.

The people question the prophet's words, accusing him of not listening to them or observing what they are doing. So the prophet must show them again and again how they are robbing God and profaning the covenant in their offerings.

He says (3:1) that God will send a messenger to prepare the way for the Savior. This man will refine them as a Refiner purifies silver or a Fuller purifies soap. He will remove their impurities, and they will bring gifts pleasing to Him (3:4). A book of remembrance will list those who fear the Lord, and in the great Day of the Lord, all will see the glory of God.

1. Read chapter 1.

a. With whom does God contrast His love for the people?

_____

b. What does God want to know from them (1:6)?

_____

c. How are they showing disrespect for God?

_____

d. What does God say in 1:11?

_____

e. In what chapter and verse do the people question God?

_____

f. Why do you think they do this?

_____

2. Read chapter 2.

a. Who does God say He will rebuke in 2:1-9?

_____

b. In 2:5, how does the God define "fear"?

_____

c. How has Judah profaned God in 2:11?

_____

d. What are they commanded to do in 2:15?

_____

e. What does the prophet say the people have done in 2:17?

_____

3. Read chapters 3-4.

a. Who will God send to the people?

_____

b. How does a refiner purify silver?

_____

c. How are the people robbing God in 3:8-9?

_____

d. How do you think this applies to Christians today?

_____

e. What is promised to those who fear God (4:2-3)?

_____

4. What have you learned from Malachi or any of the other prophetic books that would make you a better disciple?

_____

_____

SUMMARY OF THE PROPHETIC BOOKS

The work of the prophets was usually a result of God's anger against the people's sin and rebellion. It is tempting to remember only God's anger and threats in these books. He exhorts and urges them to follow Him or to repent if they have wandered. The message of the prophets is filled with great emotion because God does want His people to perish in their sins.

We must remember that each of the Major and Minor Prophets also contains God's promise of grace and mercy if they will *"Return to the Lord!"* such as the prophets called for in Jeremiah 3, Hosea 6 and Joel 2. The prophets were there to announce God's love and mercy, not just His judgment.

In this respect there is much to be learned from these sixteen Old Testament books inspired by the Holy Spirit. Their message is not really old at all, but as new as the day when we realize we, too, have wandered from God and need to follow Him in faith once again.

Their words may seem old, but their message is not. God wants us to trust Him, because He wants what is best for us. May we ever give thanks for all of God's Word in the Holy Bible, including these sixteen precious books written to call wayward people back into a closer relationship of faith and trust with Him.

+ Rev. Robert L. Tasler, 2014 +

Robert L. Tasler

Rev. Robert L. Tasler is a native of Windom, Minnesota, and a career pastor in the Lutheran Church-Missouri Synod, a conservative Lutheran body in fellowship with dozens of similar churches around the world. A 1971 ordained graduate of Concordia Seminary, St. Louis, Missouri, Pastor Bob has served parishes in North Dakota, California, Utah and Colorado.

He and his wife Carol are retired and divide their time between Colorado and Arizona. They are parents of Brian, a Denver business executive in a non-profit organization, and Chuck and his wife Debbie, Christian Day School Teachers in Phoenix, as well as proud grandparents of three.

The author's works are listed in the front of this book and can be found in detail at: http://www.bobtasler.com.

Printed in Great Britain
by Amazon

86341736R00047